Erik Satie

Ornella Volta

Erik Satie

Translated from the French
by Simon Pleasance

POCK ET  ARCHIVES
HAZAN

Cover: Erik Satie in 1923.
Photograph by Jeanne-Louise Guérin.

© Éditions Hazan, Paris, 1997
© Archives de la Fondation Erik Satie
for all the illustrative material
Editor: Éric Reinhardt
Design: Atalante
Production: Muriel Landsperger
Color separation: Seleoffset, Torino
Printing: Milanostampa, Farigliano

ISBN: 2 85025 565 3
Printed in Italy

Contents

Erik Satie in Brighton, 1867.

The Composer and his Masks

Erik Satie died on July 1, 1925, at the age of 59, in room no. 4 of the Armand-Heine ward of St. Joseph's Hospital. A room which had been procured for him by Count Etienne de Beaumont. After his death, his closest friends, the composer Darius Milhaud and the painters André Derain and Georges Braque, who had taken turns staying at his bedside during his lengthy illness, realized all of a sudden that they knew nothing whatsoever about the family ties and private life of this confirmed bachelor. A man who had never so much as opened the door of his abode to a soul – except, so rumor had it, the odd stray dog. In compliance with the law governing such cases, seals were accordingly affixed to the said door – no. 15, second floor right of the "House with Four Chimneys," at 22 rue Cauchy, in Arcueil, on the southern outskirts of Paris. The rooms behind it thus re-mained out-of-bounds for a few weeks more. Authorization to remove the seals was not granted until September 10, 1925. This was done by Mr. Gaston Viveron, clerk of the magistrate's court of the District of Gentilly, in the presence of a brother of the deceased, Mr. Conrad Satie, who had been run to earth by way of an announcement published in the press, and a notary, Maître Watin-Anguard, representing their sister Olga, who had emigrated to Argentina without leaving a forwarding address.

When the door was opened it revealed a startling sight. The living quarters had no running water, no gas for lighting, and no other such modern conveniences. The sole window with its filthy panes was now impossible to prise open. A huge spider's web sprawled over several layers of goods and chattels, heaped one on top of the other and defying description. Above this clutter there floated a folding metal cot with no sheets; two pianos with their pedals trussed up with string, the first of which, with its key board hard against the wall, housed beneath its lid a pile of unopened mail; several velvet suits, stacked one on top of the other, all identical and moth-eaten; dozens of starched detachable collars and umbrellas, some of which still had the wrapping paper from the time of their purchase; pictures darkened by their patina, but more or less protected from the dust by hoods made of newspaper; and, last of all, meticulously arrayed in cigar boxes, thousands of tiny, immaculate sheets of paper, all handwritten in black and red Indian ink. When these florid arabesques were deciphered, they yielded up pains-takingly detailed descriptions of such things as a make-believe castle, a non-existent religious order and an unplayable musical instrument.

Over the next few days, as this room was emptied so that it could be handed back to the landlord, who was now keen to let it to another tenant, two cartloads of rubbish were taken off to the garbage dump. The few identifiable objects, includ-ing the pictures, which, once cleaned, had revealed signatures of renown, were sold by roadside auction on the pavement of rue Cauchy. The many handwritten notebooks containing unpublished compositions were entrusted to Darius Milhaud, who, some years later, would share them out between the Conservatoire National de Musique in Paris and the safe of an American patron. With the exception of a few odds and ends, handed out to his closest friends, the other papers of the deceased – writings, drawings, photos, correspondence – were kept by Conrad Satie, and eventu-ally destroyed by thieves when he died.

* * *

The fact that, in his lifetime, Satie had systematically barred entry to his abode to all and sundry, had already greatly intrigued his entourage. The discovery of where he lived, once he had departed hence, did not shed any brighter light on the mystery; it served, rather, to further thicken the plot.

How could the man who, by day, was the darling of the most elegant salons return, each night, to inhabit such a lair?

How did this figure, invariably dressed to the nines, with his bowler hat and umbrella from London, his spotless stiff collar and his crisp shirt-front – almost a caricature of the respectable and conscientious civil servant – manage to emerge each and every morning from this hovel, like a pretty butterfly hatching from a shapeless larva?

And how, in the midst of such a shambles did he manage to achieve these calligraphic feats, worthy of a Benedictine monk, which he would either mail to his friends or keep, miraculously intact, in his home?

How, above all else, is it possible to reconcile the dreary, sinister atmosphere of the room in Arcueil – swiftly christened by Cocteau as "the room of the crime" – with the planetary serenity, at times leavened by zany humor, of the music which had been composed within it?

* * *

After the death of the composer, his music passed through a long period of purgatory. Homage was paid to it from time to time by the most talented of the musicians who had interpreted it – loyal to its memory, but, on the whole, having scant influence on the taste of the day. Even the slim biography which the young son of the mayor of Arcueil had written in the early 1930s, endowing his subject with precisely the right tone and flavor, could do little to parry the indifference, not to say hostility, of his constant adversaries: the *Académies*, old and new.

A good quarter of a century would elapse before, on the other side of the Atlantic, well removed from the cliquey bickering in France, the discovery was made of the profound – and we might also add, exemplary – link between the musical language of Erik Satie and the forms of artistic expression which best represent our 20th century. In the wake of the music critic of *The New York Herald Tribune*, Virgil Thomson, a survivor of that Paris of the 1920s, an as yet unknown American musician, John Cage, appointed himself the spokesman of this rediscovery.

Little by little, and not least by dint of his natural charisma, Cage managed to introduce Satie's work to younger generations around the world. First of all in the United States, and then in France and elsewhere, record publishers were quick to make up for lost time. People swiftly realized that, just as the radio which enlarged its scope, this medium, so suited to solitary listening, was particularly appropriate to a composer such as Satie. For rather than targeting the blanket concert-going public, Satie had always addressed himself, in a certain way, to one listener at a time.

So people gradually began to gauge an oeuvre which was far more complex than the so-called authorized circles had led people to believe – an oeuvre which included the *Gymnopédies*, "ancient dances" and *Relâche**, a "instantaneist ballet", *La belle Excentrique*, a "serious fantasy" and *Socrate*, a "symphonic drama", a *Messe des pauvres* designed to "heighten the intensity of our prayers" and the *Musique d'ameublement* which is played "so as not to be heard."

People were then anxious to know more about the author of this oeuvre. They wanted to understand how he had managed to appear at once urbane and misanthropic, how he could be linked, alternately, with the Rosicrucians and with Dada, and how his aesthetic range could have encompassed Puvis de Chavannes and Picasso. The bibliography

---

* English versions of the titles of Satie's works can be found page 190.

of the composer, hitherto as good as non-existent, started
to swell from the 1970s onward, at an ever brisker pace. Erik
Satie's writings were collected, his methods of composition
scrutinized and analyzed, and light was shed on his rela-
tionships and collaborations with painters, poets, and chore-
ographers. Bit by bit, the pieces of the puzzle which had
been scattered to the four corners of the earth by the dis-
mantling of the room in Arcueil is thus in the process of
being put together again.

However, rather than coming up with answers, the image
which is gradually being reconstructed is raising new ques-
tions. Contradictions, which used to take people by surprise, are not only being confirmed, but almost seem to be
staking their claim to a peaceful co-existence. It is becoming increasingly clear that, instead of trying to solve, work
out, and reconcile impulses which are generally regarded
as incompatible, Satie calmly accepted and assumed them,
as if he had reckoned that this was the ransom of the age,
if not the ransom of the human condition, period.

The modernity of Erik Satie resides, undoubtedly and quite
specifically, in this lucidity, this wisdom, and this straight-
forwardness, as applied to himself. This might also explain,
at least in part, why his work still strikes us as being topi-
cal and fresh.

* * *

In the collective imagination, the figure of Erik Satie is
inseparable from his music. But few creative people have
endeavored as much as he to rid their works of all trace of

subjectivity. The better to sidestep any explicit – or implicit – allusion to his private life, Satie went as far as to virtually forbid himself from having any such thing. To do this, he turned his person, his everyday behaviour and even his physical appearance into a banner, to some extent, of his oeuvre. And to such a degree that it is possible to follow quite closely the development of his aesthetic concerns through the various characters which he embodied turn by turn, the way an actor plays his parts in the theater.

This is what we intend to do in this small book, insomuch as we cannot actually play his music in it. This task has been considerably simplified for us by the fact that each part that Satie took on instantly caught the eye of painters, caricaturists and photographers. Painters, who, we are assured by the composer, "taught him music much better than musicians," were the first to find in Satie a model of choice. In the last decade of the 19th century, there was virtually no Salon which did not feature one or two portraits of Erik Satie among the year's crop of works, which Parisian artists in those days had the custom of exhibiting.

As far as caricaturists were concerned, they were quickly inspired by Satie's unusual figure as soon as it cut its dash on the heights of Montmartre, but they had their field day during the latter year's of the composer's life, when Satie's silhouette achieved the changelessness of a mask.

The popularization, at the turn of the century, of snapshot photography, which would put a Kodak camera into almost every household, had the effect of spawning many more opportunities for freezing Satie's image – either alone, or among a circle of friends. All the more so because he

Erik Satie at about 8 years old while at the college in Honfleur, *circa* 1874.

himself went along with it in a spirit of obvious obliging-
ness, if not connivance. Satie also took it upon himself to
go and pose in a photographer's studio to mark each "event"
in his life, such as when he was honored by being named
an *Officier d'Académie*, or for his début with the Ballets Russes,
or, again, on the day he wore his first dinner jacket.

He was at his happiest when the camera was in the hands
of artists such as his great friends Man Ray and Brancusi.
He was even more delighted, if that were possible, when
a motion picture camera was used as René Clair did in the
filmed interval of his ballet *Relâche*. Clair was so struck by
his icon that, in this same *Entr'acte*, he not only had fun
rigging out a tutu-clad dancer in an "*à la Satie*" head (complete with goatee and pince-nez), but he also turned the
composer's double – played by the actor Paul Ollivier –
into a sort of "mascot" in almost all the subsequent films
he made.

* * *

Erik Satie's friends always wondered where such an oddball
character might have come from.

For Debussy, he was "a gentle, medieval musician astray in
this century." For the draughtsman George Auriol, who was
associated with the cabaret *Le Chat Noir*, he was a sort of
Puck "come from the North in a leather coracle manned by
a crew of trolls."

In his autobiographical writings, to which he gave the title
Mémoires d'un amnésique, and not without reason, Satie did
not really offer up any more convincing leads:

*"The origins of the Saties possibly date back to the remotest of
times. Yes. More than that I can neither confirm nor deny.
I suppose, however, that this family did not belong to the Nobility
(even of the Pope), that its members were good and modest persons at everyone's beck and call – which, in former times, was
an honor and a pleasure (for the kindly lord of the lackey, needless to add). Yes.
I do not know what the Saties did during the Hundred Year's War;
nor do I have any information about their attitude to and the
part they played in the Thirty Year's War (one of our finest wars).
May the memory of my old forbears rest in peace. Yes . . .
As far as I myself am concerned, I was born in Honfleur
(Calvados), in the Pont-l'Evêque district, on May 17, 1866 . . .
I remained in that town until the age of 12 (1878) at which point
I settled in Paris. I had a nondescript childhood and an ordinary
adolescence, without any salient features worthy of being described
in serious writings. So I shall not talk about them . . ."*

Three photos – the only pictures of him, without a doubt,
over which he did not have control – document that chunk
of his life which Satie had no desire to discuss. The first
photo shows us a baby of about one, dressed as a little girl,
as was the custom of the day. With wavy, fair hair and a
wan, mocking smile, he is holding a flower in his hand in
a cardboard set, also decorated with flowers. The photo is
signed "Studio Lombardi," in Brighton, a town where the
infant Satie had undoubtedly been taken to spend his first
summer holiday with his mother, Jane Leslie Anton, an
English woman of Scottish descent.

In the second photo, the smile has vanished. It shows a slightly
distraught lad, wearing a schoolboy's uniform. After the

Erik Satie at the Conservatoire National de Musique et de Déclamation, *circa* 1884.

untimely death of his mother, when he was just six years old, his father, the Norman ship-broker Alfred Satie, went traveling to overcome his grief, entrusting his children to his family in Honfleur. His grandparents wasted no time in getting the young Eric to renounce the Anglican religion in which his mother had raised him, so that he could be given a Catholic baptism. They then sent him as a boarder to a "college" (which would later be named after his friend Alphonse Allais) which stood just a stone's throw from their house. The boy obtained no more than a certificate of merit in "vocal music" at the high school and he was called *Crin-crin* (literally squeaky fiddle). He was given piano lessons with the organist at St. Leonard's church in Honfleur, one Mr. Vinot, who composed polkas and waltzes between services.

Eric (only later on in his life would he change the last letter of his first name to a "k" to emphasize his Viking origins) is not smiling in the third photo either. The young ladies in his entourage nicknamed him "the serious man," to boot. The fact is that this bespectacled teenager did not have much to be happy about. Living in Paris from the age of twelve, he attended the Conservatoire National de Musique et de Déclamation, deriving no pleasure from his classes and obtaining no noteworthy results. He had been enrolled here by his father's second wife, Mrs. Eugénie Barnetche, an academically trained pianist and composer, with whom he had a lukewarm relationship. It was she, nevertheless, who, during a concert tour in Russia, was the first to play a work by her stepson in a concert hall.

But everything at this juncture was poised to change, as we learn from a later passage in *Mémoires d'un amnésique*:

"After a somewhat brief adolescence I turned into an ordinarily passible young man, no more. It was at this point in my life that I started to think and write musically.

What a tiresome idea! A most tiresome idea! . . .

Indeed, for in no time I was making use of an (original) originality that was disagreeable, untimely, anti-French, unnatural, etc . . ."

The moment when Satie started to "think and write musically" – the moment when, in some ways, he authorizes us to take an interest in him – overlapped with his début into society. In his undoubted quest for an audience that suited him, when he came of age (1887) he left the family house and set up home in Montmartre which, at that time, was "the land of painters and poets." It was also the land of "eccentrics," for all those people who could no longer identify with the social background of their birth, be they provincial, middle-class or upper middle-class, seemed to have passed the word among themselves to gravitate towards that place where they could openly display their (original . . .) originality with complete impunity.

Their main haunt was the cabaret called *Le Chat Noir*, where musicians earned a living – or, at the very least, their daily glass of absinthe – by accompanying shadow theater performances on the harmonium, and where poets went to recite their poems on a podium, which so accustomed them to the footlights that they would no longer be able to do without them. As for painters, they decorated the bistros which fed them and also practised the art of the poster, quite unashamedly. At that time, advertising was still regarded, as Blaise Cendrars tells us, as "one of the seven wonders of the modern world," because of the unbridled fantasies which it permitted and because of the direct contact with the street which it finally offered to artists, hitherto bogged down in subjects imposed from on high by the Academies and by the conventional tastes of the "élite" who frequented the salons.

Satie is perhaps the very first artist to have the idea of using this medium not by calling on his brush or his pen to launch some product or other, but in order to get his own works known. Accordingly, on November 24, 1888, he published the following announcement in the magazine put out by *Le Chat Noir* to bolster its prestige among the capital's intellectual circles:

"Erik Satie's 3rd Gymnopédie has just been published, at 66 boulevard Magenta.

To the musical public, we cannot recommend this essentially artistic work too highly. It is a work which rightly stands among the most beautiful of the century in which this unfortunate gentleman was born."

The very title of the work thus announced seemed to be devised deliberately to attract the attention of the most world-wearily indifferent of readers. Satie was so acutely aware of this that, from his first visit to *Le Chat Noir*, he declared himself to be a *"gymnopédiste"* – and this was well before the composition which would, so to speak, explain this term, had seen the light of day. With just one single word, he thus demonstrated that he was qualified to join a coterie which did not admit any run-of-the-mill mortal. At the same time, he let it be known that he identified himself wholly with the music within him.

It was not just the title which set the *Gymnopédies* apart from what was being produced at that time. While most of his colleagues were busily following the path mapped out by Wagner under the beguiling name of "music of the future," Erik Satie, for his part, was intent upon conjuring up the music that predated Wagnerism: Romanticism, the Baroque and even Gregorian plainsong. In a word, he would endeavor to bring back the forgotten sounds of Greek Antiquity.

One of the constant features of our composer, throughout his life, was a far-reaching interest in the vanished past (a yearning, perhaps, for Paradise Lost?). But this interest was compounded by an acute awareness of the impossibility of regaining this past as it was perceived by those who had actually experienced and lived it. His *Gymnopédies* thus in no way claimed to recreate the melodies to which the γυμνοι πατδεζ or "naked children" danced in Sparta in honor of Apollo. Rather, they would express a nostalgia for the bare acoustic setting in which those children danced. Far from wishing to restore those temples of yore and their rituals, his intent was to rediscover that childhood of art which did not depend for its expression on any plethora of means.

When Satie realized that this was not self-evident for all and sundry, and in particular for his friends at *Le Chat Noir*, who, without casting too quizzical an eye, had started to call him "the Greek musician," he had the idea of pushing his identification with his oeuvre to its utmost limit. Starting with the most conspicuous – in the real meaning of the term – aspect, his physical appearance: *"One day,"* we learn from one of his friends, *"he took his clothes, rolled them up into a ball, sat on them, dragged them across the floor, trampled on them,*

*sprayed them with all kinds of liquids, until he had reduced them
to nothing less than tatters. He stove in his hat, wrecked his shoes,
ripped his tie, and replaced his underwear with awful flannelette
shirts. He stopped tending to his beard and let his hair grow."*

People who waited to see him on the Montmartre stage,
where the picturesque was the norm, clad in a linen tunic
and wearing sandals on his feet, in the manner of a figure
such as Raymond Duncan, but well ahead of the times, thus
discovered in his stead a stirring *Monsieur le Pauvre* or Mister
Pauper, displaying his poverty with the greatest dignity.
Satie did not "doll up" any of his works, and he systematically turned his back on any form of compromise with
money, up until the day he died, so he would never fail that
nickname, be it in his art or in his life.

* * *

On February 9, 1889, the magazine of *Le Chat Noir* announced the advent of a new work by *"The indefatigable Erik
Satie, sphinx man and wooden-headed* [as in having a wooden
leg, ed.] *composer . . . a suite of melodies written in the mystico-
liturgical genre which the Author idolizes with the suggestive
title, the* Ogives *. . ."*

The witty tone of his announcement possibly took people
aback in relation to the "mystico-liturgical" genre that it
claimed to herald. This was neither the first nor the last
time that Satie had fun misleading his inexpert and absent-
minded readers, for the only thing that really concerned
him was being understood by people who were on the same
wave-length as he.

His brother Conrad, for example – at that time his closest confidant – knew that, far from being in the vein of some Montmartre hoodwink, Satie had composed those *Ogives* after spending many long hours contemplating the ribbed vaults of Notre-Dame. Contemplation of this Gothic cathedral, which had been considerably restored in the 19th century by Viollet-le-Duc, could only be instructive for a composer who was keen to "restore" the sounds of bygone times with the means of the day.

Another reason for this contemplation on the part of the man who would, before long, invite a new nickname – *Esotérik Satie* – lay in that heretical tradition to which he was undoubtedly privy, whereby the ambiguous name of "Notre Dame" paid homage not to the Virgin Mary of Catholic worship, but to the Egyptian goddess, Isis. According to this same tradition, *Is-is* is merely an onomatopoeic word suggesting the crackling of sacred fire, just as the pointed arch (the ogive) and the pyramid represent the stylized image of a flame.

Two years later, a chance encounter would lead to the blossoming of this soft spot for esotericism which already lurked within our composer.

During a chat about everything and nothing at the corner of a bar (or, more probably, in front of that window of the Librairie de l'Art Indépendant – the Independent Art Bookshop – on rue Chaussée d'Antin, which hid rather displayed books on the occult), the Sâr Joséphin Péladan, Grand Master of the Rosicrucians, discovered that the young unknown musician shared his lofty ideals ("just as Religion has become art to speak to the masses, so Art must become religion to speak to the minority"). On the spur of the moment, he appointed him chapelmaster of his order. Here, Satie came upon his first chance to have his music heard in public and, what is more, in select settings: the church of St. Germain l'Auxerrois, first and foremost, where the kings of France had been baptized, and which the Sâr was now making use of to launch his first *Geste esthétique*; next, a Salon of symbolist painting, where this *Geste* took the form of a Festival of Poetry, Music and Theater, and was spread over several evenings.

Engrossed by his new responsibilities, our chapelmaster started by unearthing appropriate clothing. Now that he had to hobnob with a man like Péladan who sported showy, out-of-date apparel (embroidered satin waistcoats, lace ruffles, thigh-length buckskin boots), and who matched his dark tousled head of hair with a Mephistophelean beard, Satie cut his blond hair into a long Nazarene-style and made his image intentionally more sombre, abandoning the Pauper's top hat and tunic for a soft-brimmed hat and a long, sober frockcoat.

Conversely, to compose the *Sonneries de la Rose+Croix*, which were to be used for inaugurating ceremonies, and the preludes of Sâr Péladan's Chaldean *"wagnerie," Le Fils des Étoiles*, star turn of the first night, he did not have to look far for the style that fitted the bill. To achieve a sacerdotal acoustic atmosphere that was "white and motionless," all he had to do was take the path blazed by the *Ogives* to its utmost limit, without, what is more, concerning himself over the taste exhibited by his patron. While the Sâr took himself for an ardent Wagnerian, he was not, in fact, enough of a musician to grasp the difference.

Here, he was not alone. Leaving aside the vehement Willy, who, in *L'Echo de Paris*, lamented the "faucet music" (so-called because of its repetitive and anti-dramatic character) of our chapelmaster, all that the audience and the critics of those evenings saw in those unusual tones was the application of Péladanesque theories. Irked by this blend which called into question that which he held most dear – the independence of his aesthetics – Satie then preferred to give up the advantages of his association with the Sâr, which he did by abruptly sundering his relationship with him.

* * *

One of Péladan's Rosicrucian rules would have the artist subscribing to a regime of chastity, so that he need never be sidetracked from the work which it was his mission to complete. To make it all the more abundantly clear that he was now branching out on his own, Satie then hastened to flaunt – for the one and only time in his life – an amorous relationship. But because of the particular temperament of his chosen partner – the "paintress" Suzanne Valadon – she would nevertheless entice him far further than was his wish, for, in his innermost being, he altogether shared the views of the Sâr on this subject.

To free himself from Suzanne, he would resort, first of all, to musical devices, by composing a *Neuvaine pour la fort tranquillité de mon âme*, and by inflicting upon himself a kind of penance, aptly named *Vexations*, which would keep him glued to his keyboard for 14 hours on the trot, by forcing him to repeat a certain melodic motif all of 840 times. There were no telling results, so he finally had the idea – far-fetched, but effective – of calling the neighborhood police and asking them to come to rid him of this over-encroaching love. Alone once again after these adventures, Satie felt the need for a bulwark against the obstacles – and temptations – of everyday life. So he founded his own Church, appointing himself its head (but also its one and only follower). This would enable him, if nothing else, to derive some advantage from a platform from which "to fight against society by means of music and painting," and hurl curses at his enemies.

He called the Church the *Eglise Métropolitaine d'Art de Jésus conducteur* [the Metropolitan Church of Art of Jesus the leader] (there are some who hold that *Jés-us* is an onomatopoeic form equivalent to *Is-is*), and set up its headquarters in the room he occupied at the very top of the hill of Montmartre, which was no larger than a "cupboard." For the ceremonies of this church, he composed the *Messe des pauvres* for organs and choirs, but he never quite managed to finish it. This title does at least attest to the fact that neither esoteric matters nor his encounters of all kinds ever removed him from his most stalwart friend, Poverty.

* * *

Most of the ecclesiastical chants, while changing the words, borrowed from popular tunes. One fine day, Satie turned away, once and for all, from music associated with genuflection. He decided to explore popular music in its own right, as it was being practised in variety shows – that arena of so-called "light" entertainment, which was on the whole looked down upon by informed musical circles.

Now he would spend the bulk of his time in cabarets and cafés with live song and dance. He accordingly abandoned his austere frockcoat for a becoming, mustard-yellow velvet suit: he bought seven identical suits, thanks to the generosity of a friend who had just come into some money. Decked out in this uniform for seven years running, he earned himself a new nickname, in English, "The Velvet Gentleman," in a Montmartre which had, meantime, turned a love of things English into a fashionable pursuit.

Having shed its liturgical restrictions, Erik Satie's music became more supple and more flowing. Without any evident connection with the work to which they referred, the mocking, flippant titles of the collections for piano which signposted this new period – *Airs à faire fuir* and *Danses de travers* at the very beginning (1897) and *Trois morceaux en forme de poire* at the very end (1903) – smacked of the eccentric spirit of his new-found friends, those cabaret artists.

It was, in fact, as a hired pianist for the cabaret artist Vincent Hyspa that our "Velvet Gentleman" would earn his livelihood, and also by composing "*rudes saloperies*" or "dirty ditties" for this latter, or else for Paulette Darty, "queen of the slow waltz." From this experience, he understood the need for, and possibly the way of, establishing a contact with his audience which classical composers were not necessarily acquainted with. In this environment he also had a chance – even if for the time being he was the only one to be aware of it – to experiment with the daring harmonics which the *Grands Concerts* were not ready to accommodate.

Satie was already pushing forty when he realized that it was high time that he pulled himself together and took stock.

Claude Debussy – the only friend with whom he had the feeling of being able to "express his meagre thoughts" – had just achieved, with his opera *Pelléas et Mélisande* (1902), the culmination of an aesthetic ideal which they had both been pursuing in tandem.

If he hoped to find himself again, there was now nothing else for it but to go back to square one.

So the erstwhile "bad pupil" enrolled in the Schola Cantorum, headed by Vincent d'Indy, to attend the counterpoint classes given by Albert Roussel, four years his senior. Here he learnt the art of the fugue, inventing, in passing, so he claims, "the modern fugue which did not exist (all for expositions)," and he called his next work, made up of two chorales and two fugues, *En Habit de Cheval*, to clearly underline that he had patiently undergone that severe discipline like a draft horse attached to a four-wheeled cart. Having become, as Debussy would taunt him, a "famous counter-pointist," at the age of 42, he was awarded the first diploma of his life by the Schola. This officially authorized him to compose music . . . twenty years after he had written the *Gymnopédies*.

His attendance at the Schola had called for yet another change of attire. This middle-aged Monsieur who shared the classroom benches with pimply teenagers chose thenceforth to assume the correct and all-purpose appearance of a small-time official: bowler hat, stiff collar and cane – this latter soon to be replaced by a black umbrella. Thus decked out, Satie also, and finally, won the respect of his fellow citizens of Arcueil – the small township on the southern outskirts of Paris where he had taken lodgings just before 1900 – who had, to begin with, been put off by the eccentric "Velvet Gentleman".

Unaware that his young son, Pierre-Daniel, would one day be the composer's first biographer, the architect Pierre-Alexandre Templier offered Satie a column in *L'Avenir d'Arcueil-Cachan*, the "radical-socialist" periodical which he edited. In it, Satie published hilarious, anonymous advertisements extolling the merits of local recreational activities: dance classes, gymnastic lessons and film courses. As a member of the *Patronage laïque* [Lay Association], he also gave free lessons in music theory to the school children whom he would take on walks on Thursdays by the classful. He also contributed personally to the "artistic matinée" programs of the *Cercle lyrique et musical arcueillais* [Lyrical and Musical Club of Arcueil], calling upon the services of his old contacts in the variety show world, Paulette Darty and Vincent Hyspa. To avoid embarrassing his neighbors on the same floor – plumbers and house painters – he presented himself to them only as a composer of popular songs. On 15 July 1909, at the proposal of the town council, he received from the Prefect of the Seine a medal issued by the Ministry of Education for "civic merit." He accepted this modest decoration with good grace, even though, throughout his life, he would make fun of persons receiving the *Légion d'Honneur*, and even deride those who refused this honor, because it was a question, above all, of "not meriting it."

Mr. Templier introduced him to politics. Satie had always avoided, before this, any involvement of which he was not the author. Now he started by joining the radical party, although he suddenly abandoned them for the socialist party, in the wake of the assassination of the founder of *L'Humanité*, Jean Jaurès. While Satie grumbled about the fact that "in art, communists are disconcertingly bourgeois," he nevertheless joined the communist party after the Congress at Tours, if only for the pleasure of having himself announced among the Right Bank aristocrats, with whom he was hobnobbing at the time, as: "Erik Satie of the Arcueil Soviet."

* * *

It was precisely when he could at last reckon on being thoroughly at one with his suburban life and environment, that, as if to his own surprise, he once again developed an interest in Parisian musical circles, as well as in the various salons in the capital where opinions were formed. Maurice Ravel, whom he had known as a teenager and whose early works he had influenced, had become sufficiently famous and powerful, by about 1910, to be able to impose on his entourage the "rediscovery," of this elderly, overlooked musician. As a result of a cannily conducted operation, whose secret aim was to weaken Debussy's prestige – at that time, for Ravel, he was the great rival to be outmatched – Satie found himself all of a sudden being celebrated as the "Precursor of modern music", and it was under this label that his music would finally be played at concerts, and duly published.

After an initial moment of thrill aroused by this unexpected turn of events, Satie would end up feeling quite cramped in this doyen-like situation in which people were keen to pigeonhole him, come what may. So he started to compose, at a frantic pace, a whole series of farfetched works, intended in the first instance, with gusts of poetic humour, to bring down the monument within which people were trying to embalm him. As the star attraction of this series, the "lyrical comedy, *Le Piège de Méduse*," by Erik Satie, with dance music by the same Gentleman" – a masterpiece of the theater of the absurd but well ahead of its time – would have to wait until the upheavals of the Great War and the blossoming of Dada in Paris before finding a theater prepared to stage it, seven years later.

In fact, the war which broke out in 1914 brought everything to a grinding halt. Publishing houses and concert halls closed down one after the other, while all the young men left for the front, from which many would never return. Marooned once again, penniless, and too old to be called up to fight, Satie hung around Montparnasse, where the artistic life which had once thrived in Montmartre had moved to some years previously. In the midst of the gaudy bohemian disarray of the artists who had stayed put (because they were foreigners, on leave or wounded), his petty official's suit – which he would wear constantly from now on – struck people as quirky and odd. It was in a painter's studio, transformed into a concert hall and exhibition gallery, to help people to carry on the artistic fight despite the adverse circumstances that our *Vieux hautbois dormant* [old sleeping oboe, a play on words with Sleeping Beauty] would

be discovered, once again, by an ambitious young poet by
the name of Jean Cocteau.

"In Paris the field was free: we moved in," Cocteau would
say, without too many qualms. He had been anxious for
some time to hit the big time on the Parisian stage, and in
Satie he saw the ideal partner. With a third accomplice,
Pablo Picasso, they tossed a bomb designed to shatter atti-
tudes of the day, at the very same moment when enemy
guns were preparing to fire on Paris.

With its absence of plot, its grotesque cardboard characters, its "orchestra of typewriters," the ballet *Parade*, by
Cocteau, Satie and Picasso, would represent the very first
example of *"art pauvre"* of the century. It was all the more
striking because it was staged – at the Théâtre du Châtelet,
on May 18, 1917 – by Diaghilev's Ballet Russes, hitherto
famed for the sumptuous spectacle of their productions.
The *"succès de scandale"* of *Parade* made Satie the target of
venomous critics, and at the same time, a "signpost" for
young musicians. Gathered together, turn by turn, under
various names – the *Nouveaux Jeunes*, the *Groupe des Six*,
the *École d'Arcueil* – these musicians would henceforth claim
to espouse his aesthetics, which were identified with an
extreme economy of means and a freedom of choice from
every point of view, turning a blind eye to academic obstacles, to the point of including music hall numbers in a classical concert.

Erik Satie then took his world by surprise one more time,
by composing the "symphonic drama" *Socrate*, based on
Plato's Dialogues, where, by going beyond them, he regain-
ed the serene beauty and the serious tone of his Rosicrucian

works. For these young musicians, the person they then referred to as "*le Bon Maître*" bore a blatant resemblance to the Greek philosopher.

* * *

But our composer had not yet uttered his last word. Before ending, in hospital, a life which had not been without its struggles and its twists and turns, he would find the time – between two other ballets, *Mercure* and *Relâche*, the one composed with Picasso, the other with Picabia – to come up with a new "consumer product," the *Musique d'ameublement* "which must be played so as not to be heard," made up of extracts – repeated ad lib – from works composed by those of his colleagues who were not dear to him (Saint-Saëns, Ambroise Thomas . . .). Just before the spread of the "wireless," Erik Satie had in fact observed the need that people were already beginning to feel for background noise to their everyday activities. As a result, he was keen to stop people squandering music which demands attention and respect for such utilitarian requirements.

By way of a swansong, he wrote the first film music, frame by frame, at a time when the cinema was still silent.

It was a quip by Francis Picabia which provided him with his very last nickname: "Erik is *Satierik.*"

Mister Pauper

"We don't savor the state of poverty enough, and this is a sign of very serious disorders."
Erik Satie

The dingy room in Arcueil, where Erik Satie would end his days, was no better furnished than his very first lodgings on the Hill of Montmartre. Sitting, to borrow his own words, "in my cupboard, by my fireless-place," he was nevertheless surrounded by prints, drawings and posters – and later by masterpieces – which attest to his avowed interest in the visual arts. Above the fireplace hung a mirror which went with him everywhere, for it was "laden with memories."

Erik Satie's apartment in Montmartre, by Santiago Rusiñol.
This was the only picture inside his rooms ever authorized by Satie.
Page 35: Erik Satie at a Montmartre cabaret, *circa* 1890.

Handwritten score of the *3rd Gymnopédie*, 1888.

MONTJOYE-MONTMARTRE

Rédaction et Administration : 13, rue Victor-Massé

PARIS, LE   188.

Le Chat Noir

Journal hebdomadaire

Portrait of Erik Satie on the headed notepaper of
the Chat Noir cabaret magazine, *circa* 1888.

Erik Satie in front of the Moulin de la Galette, by Ramón Casas, detail, 1891.

Sign in ancient French and uncial lettering affixed by Erik Satie to the door of his apartment, offering to hire out his melodies to curious passers-by.

Erik Satie playing the harmonium for the Shadow Theater at Le Chat Noir by Santiago Rusiñol, 1891.

Zinc cut-out for the Shadow Theater at Le Chat Noir,
from a drawing by Henri Rivière.

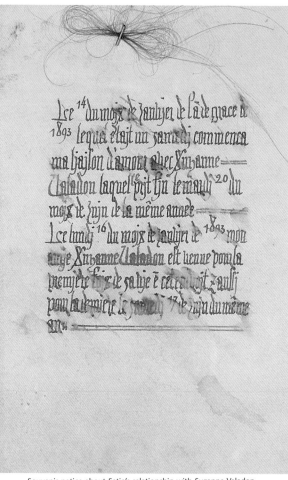

Le 14 du mois de Janvier de l'an de grace à
1893 lequel était un samedi commença
ma liaison d'amour avec Suzanne
Valadon laquel prit fin le mardi 20 du
mois de Juin de la même année
Le lundi 16 du mois de Janvier de 1893 mon
ange Suzanne Valadon est venue pour la
première fois de sa vie è cela a été aussi
pour la dernière le mardi 17 de Juin du même
an

Souvenir notice about Satie's relationship with Suzanne Valadon,
complete with a lock of her hair, and smudged by his own tears,
put up by Satie in his lodgings.

Suzanne Valadon with her son Maurice Utrillo and a dog held on
a lead by Erik Satie. She snipped Satie out of the photograph,
to shield her memories from prying eyes.

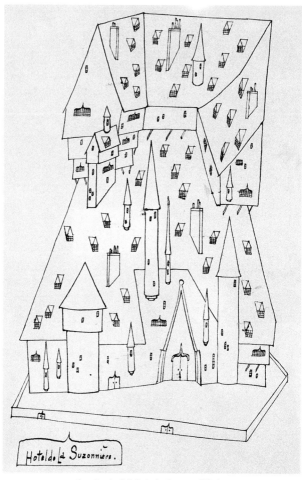

Hotel de La Suzonnière.

Drawing by Erik Satie for Suzanne Valadon.
All that Mister Pauper could offer his lady friend were paper castles.

Portrait of Erik Satie by Suzanne Valadon, detail, 1893.

Letter from Erik Satie to Suzanne Valadon ("Biqui"), dated March 11, 1893.
Here it is Satie's name and address which the recipient cut from
the only letter she ever received from him.

Portrait of Valadon by Satie, 1893.

Santiago Rusiñol, *Love Song*, detail, 1893.
This is the only document where Erik Satie and Suzanne Valadon
are shown together.

Esotérik Satie

*"An ogival and gymnopaedic
musician whom I called
– o, witty me! –
Esotérik Satie."*
Alphonse Allais

Erik Satie by Antoine de La Rochefoucauld, 1894.
Page 53: Félicien Rops, *The Rare Fish*. Seal of the Librairie de l'Art independent,
which published Erik Satie's earliest booklets.

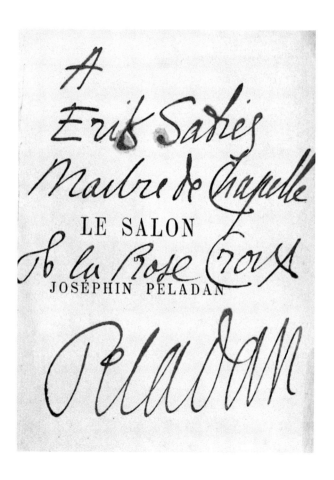

Dedication by the Sâr Péladan on a copy of his book
Le Salon de Péladan in 1891: "À Erik Satie, maître de chapelle de la Rose+Croix"
["To Erik Satie, chapelmaster of the Rosicrucians"].

Erik Satie by Paul Signac, *circa* 1892.

Score by Erik Satie published by the Rosicrucians in 1892.
Cover with a red chalk drawing by Puvis de Chavannes.

Erik Satie doing battle with the symbols of Wagnerism
extolled by the Rosicrucians.

Organ-gargoyle drawn by Erik Satie for an imaginary cathedral.

✝ Messire ERIK SATIE ✝
Parcier & Maître de chapelle de
l'Eglise Métropolitaine d'Art
de Jesuf Conducteur,

6, Rue Cortot,

PARIS.

A self-addressed envelope to "Messire Erik Satie, *Parcier* and chapelmaster
of the Metropolitan Church of Art of Jesus the Leader." Parcier is an old word for
"*partiaire*" or shareholder, chosen by Satie to let it be known that he regarded
himself as the sharecropper of God.

The *Parcier* of the Metropolitan Church of Art, *circa* 1895.

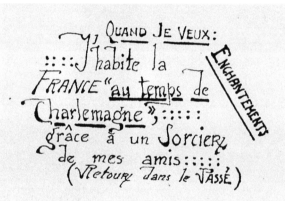

One of the secret dreams which Satie left notes about among
the thousands of hand-written scraps and jottings which he never showed to
a soul while he was alive.

Erik Satie painted "in the middle of the street, in fierce rain"
by Ignacio Zuloaga, 1891.

Erik Satie by Marcellin Desboutin.
The hands of the young Satie as a conscript *(right)* have the same pose
required for the esoteric rites of the *Parcier* wearing a cassock *(left)*.

The farewell to "kneeling music" was symbolized by this *Verset laïque et somptueux,* a Contemporary Composer's Autographs Collection exhibed at the 1900 World Fair.

The Velvet Gentleman

*"Let's not forget what we owe
to the Music Hall and
the Circus . . . The Music
Hall and the Circus have
an innovative spirit."*
Erik Satie

A. Grass-Mick, *Moving House*, 1897. The "Velvet Gentleman" and
two of his friends are pushing a cart laden with furniture along rue Lepic.
Page 69: Erik Satie, *circa* 1897.

As the century drew to a close, Satie moved to Arcueil, in the southern suburbs of Paris, but he continued to frequent the cabarets of Montmartre. This meant a daily trek, on foot, of some 12.5 miles.

The Chat Noir composer Georges Fragerolle seated
between Debussy and Satie, *circa* 1898.

Erik Satie, 1898.

Jane Avril at the Bal Tabarin, in a picture by A. Grass-Mick.
Erik Satie is among the onlookers, on the left.
Opposite: Erik Satie in a *guinguette* or open air café, *circa* 1896.

Satie bought seven identical velvet suits
complete with matching hats, which he would wear uninterruptedly for seven
years. It was this that earned him the nickname of "Velvet Gentleman."

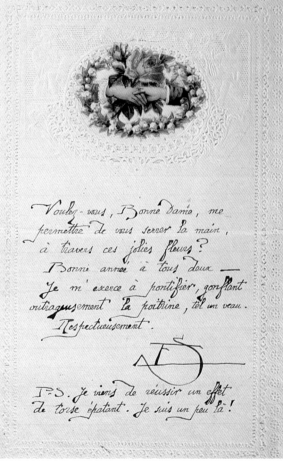

Voulez-vous, Bonne Dame, me
permettre de vous serrer la main,
à travers ces jolies fleurs ?
Bonne année à tous deux —
Je m'exerce à pontifier, gonflant
outrageusement la poitrine, tel un veau.
Respectueusement.

ɛS̄

P̄.S̄. Je viens de réussir un effet
de torse épatant. Je suis un peu là !

Letter from Erik Satie to the "queen of the slow waltz," Paulette Darty.

Publicity postcard of the publishers Bellon, Ponscarme & Cie for Erik Satie's "sung waltz" *Je te veux*, which was in Paulette Darty's repertoire.

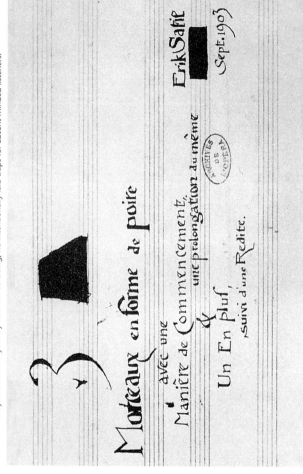

Handwritten manuscript of the *Trois morceaux en forme de poire*. Erik Satie spent a good deal of time with *chansonniers* (satirical cabaret performers), and this prompted him to give his works witty titles, even when they were not very funny at all. In so doing, he intentionally laid traps for absent-minded listeners.

Satie, eating with friends in their home: "I behave better at table than in the saddle," he would say.

A. Grass-Mick, *Au Café des Princes*, 1898. On the left, Toulouse-Lautrec and Jane Avril, with Erik Satie. On the right, facing, Georges Courteline wearing a trilby.

A. Grass-Mick, *Au Lapin agile*, 1905. Seated around the owner Frédé are Poulbot, Roland Dorgelès and Romain Rolland, with Erik Satie on the right, beside Jehan Rictus.

Erik Satie in good company, *circa* 1898.

Publicity postcard of the Brasseries parisiennes, with Erik Satie, wearing a boater, sitting outside.

Erik Satie's first draft of the "sung march" *La Diva de l'Empire,* 1904.

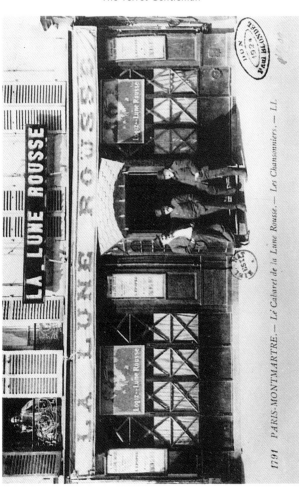

1791 PARIS-MONTMARTRE. — Le Cabaret de la Lune Rousse. — Les Chansonniers. — LL.

Postcard in the *Les Chansonniers* series: Numa Blès and Dominique Bonnaud, song writers of *La Diva de l'"Empire,"* and Erik Satie. The "Velvet Gentleman" is wearing a bowler hat, heralding the next sartorial style he would adopt.

Mr. Satie, Composer

"My name is Erik Satie,
like everyone else."
Erik Satie

Imaginary plan of Arcueil drawn by Erik Satie.
Page 87: Erik Satie, 1909.

The *House with Four Chimneys*, in Arcueil, where Satie spent the last 30 years
of his life in a room with no modern conveniences.

The Lay Association of Arcueil-Cachan, 1908.
"Mr. Satie, composer," is standing second from the left between
"Mr. Veyssière, house painter" and "Mr. Templier, architect," father of
the composer's biographer-to-be. Satie was only accepted by

the people of Arcueil when he traded his bohemian garb for
the uniform of a minor official – bowler hat, stiff collar and umbrella.
On behalf of the Lay Association, he took the children in the local schools
for walks on Thursdays and organized their recreational activities.

Haunted by the His Master's Voice dog, Erik Satie played the piano at
the children's ball in Arcueil. Drawing by Nick Cudworth.

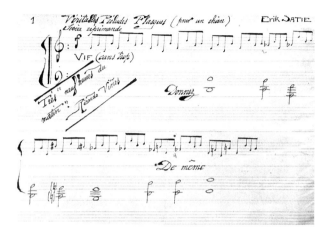

Handwritten manuscript of "*Véritables préludes flasques (pour un chien)*" 1912.
Erik Satie's visiting card which he designed himself.

Invitation for a reception given by the people of Arcueil in honour of Erik Satie,
when he was appointed *Officier d'Académie* "for civic merit" in 1909.

The Montmartre *chansonnier* Vincent Hyspa (right) went to enliven the
"artistic matinées" in Arcueil-Cachan, at the request of his old friend Erik Satie.
Drawing by Zyg Brunner.

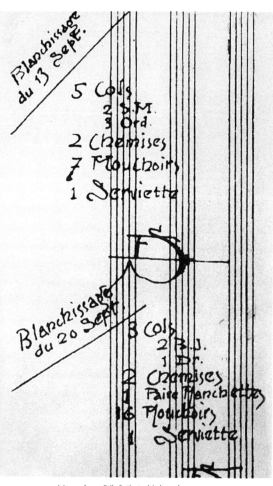

Memo from Erik Satie to his laundress.
Opposite: "Mr. Satie" sporting his decoration on his lapel, 1909.

The Forerunner

"I have learnt to see into the distance, the far distance . . . the future proves me right. Haven't I always been a good prophet?"
Erik Satie

Erik Satie, *circa* 1911.
Page 99: Erik Satie photographed in about 1912 by Carol-Bérard, chairman of the Musician's Union, to which Satie belonged.

Schola Cantorum

ÉCOLE SUPÉRIEURE DE MUSIQUE

269, Rue Saint-Jacques, à Paris

ANNÉE 1908

Diplôme de Sortie de Classe

1er DEGRÉ

Nous soussignés, constatons que Monsieur
Satie, Erik,
élève du cours de Contrepoint,
a satisfait aux examens de fin d'année avec la mention
Très-bien et qu'il remplit les conditions requises
pour se livrer exclusivement à l'étude de la Composition.

En foi de quoi nous lui avons délivré le présent diplôme.

Fait à Paris, à la Schola Cantorum,

le 15 Juin 1908

SIGNÉ :
Vincent d'Indy
Directeur des Études de la Schola.

SIGNÉ :
Secrétaire général.

SIGNÉ :
Albert Roussel
Professeur de la Classe.

Erik Satie's diploma from the Schola Cantorum, signed by
Vincent d'Indy and Albert Roussel, 1908.

Satie clearly showed his acute desire to be generally accepted by adopting the uniform of a minor official. In this same vein, now pushing 40, the erstwhile dunce went back to school and was awarded his first diploma, from the Schola Cantorum in 1908.

While he was preparing to try out his new-found knowledge, Maurice Ravel unexpectedly rediscovered Satie's youthful works and made Satie known among musical circles as a "forerunner" of the new tendencies, which, at that time, were embodied by Ravel himself and Debussy. Debussy took this badly and his hitherto special and happy relationship with Satie took a turn for the worse. When Satie visited this old friend, our composer was henceforth consigned to the children's room, which did not irk him in the least: "I'll have you know that children are younger than plenty of old fogeys," he observed. Satie abandoned both his former ways (just when these were finally gaining recognition and fame) and the strict discipline of the Schola by which he had forced himself to abide. In so doing, Satie gave free rein to his poetic wit by producing a whole host of small, whimsical, fantasia-like pieces. He also published his disconcerting *Mémoires d'un amnésique* in a music magazine.

Claude Debussy and Erik Satie photographed by Igor Stravinsky, 1910.

Erik Satie with Debussy and the young Tosti Russel.

Erik Satie with Dolly Bardac, daughter from Mrs. Debussy's first marriage, and Sheridan and Tosti Russel, children of the director of the Boston Opera House.

Erik Satie wearing a boater in Debussy's garden.

Mémoires d'un amnésique.

CE QUE JE SUIS (Fragment).

Tout le monde vous dira que je ne suis pas un musicien.[1] C'est juste.

Dès le début de ma carrière, je me suis, de suite, classé parmi les phonométrographes. Mes travaux sont de la pure phonométrique. Que l'on prenne les " Fils des Étoiles " ou les " Morceaux en forme de poire ", " En habit de Cheval " ou les " Sarabandes ", on perçoit qu'aucune idée musicale n'a présidé à la création de ces œuvres. C'est la pensée scientifique qui domine.

Du reste, j'ai plus de plaisir à mesurer un son que j'en ai à l'entendre. Le phonomètre à la main, je travaille joyeusement et sûrement.

Que n'ai-je pesé ou mesuré ? Tout de Beethoven, tout de Verdi, etc. C'est très curieux.

La première fois que je me servis d'un phonoscope, j'examinai un si bémol de moyenne grosseur. Je n'ai, je vous assure, jamais vu chose plus répugnante. J'appelai mon domestique pour le lui faire voir.

Au phono-peseur un fa dièse ordinaire, très commun, atteignit 93 kilogrammes. Il émanait d'un fort gros ténor dont je pris le poids.

Connaissez-vous le nettoyage des sons ? C'est assez sale. Le filage est plus propre ; savoir les classer est très minutieux et demande une bonne vue. Ici nous sommes dans la phonotechnique.

Quant aux explosions sonores, souvent si désagréables, le coton, fixé dans les oreilles, les atténue, pour soi, convenablement. Ici, nous sommes dans la pyrophonie.

Pour écrire mes " Pièces Froides ", je me suis servi d'un caléidophone-enregistreur. Cela prit sept minutes. J'appelai mon domestique pour les lui faire entendre.

Je crois pouvoir dire que la phonologie est supérieure à la musique. C'est plus varié. Le rendement pécuniaire est plus grand. Je lui dois ma fortune.

En tout cas, au motodynamophone, un phonométreur médiocrement exercé peut, facilement, noter plus de sons que ne le fera le plus habile musicien, dans le même temps, avec le même effort. C'est grâce à cela que j'ai tant écrit.

L'avenir est donc à la philophonie.

ERIK SATIE

[1] Voir : O. Séré, *Musiciens français d'aujourd'hui* p. 138.

Ce que je suis, a "fragment" from the *Mémoires d'un amnésique*,
Revue musicale S. I. M., April 15, 1912.

The Old
Sleeping Oboe

*"Satie hides behind his
pince-nez, behind his hand,
behind his pranks . . . "*
Jean Cocteau

Arvin Fougstedt, *The Salle Huyghens*, 1916. In the background,
Picasso, Ortiz de Zarate, Renée Gros and Moïse Kisling. In the centre,
the art dealers Gustaf Ellstrom and Léopold Zborowski.
Page 109: Erik Satie by Jean Cocteau.

£209.36 9/2

LYRE ET PALETTE
6, RUE HUYGHENS (XIVᵉ)
Carrefour Raspail et Montparnasse

1ᴿᴱ EXPOSITION

MATISSE, PICASSO, ORTIZ DE ZARATE
MODIGLIANI, KISLING

Vernissage : Dimanche 19 Novembre 1916, à 2 heures

A 3 heures :

INSTANT MUSICAL
ŒUVRES D'ERIK SATIE

Mᵈ Jacques Doucet

Invitation sent to patron of the arts Jacques Doucet for the opening
of the *1st Exhibition* in rue Huyghens, with an *Instant musical* by Erik Satie.
Many galleries and theaters were closed because of the war, so artists
– and artistes – gathered in a disused studio on rue Huyghens, in Montparnasse.
Valentine Gross (the future Valentine Hugo) took Cocteau to this meeting place
where he discovered Erik Satie, who had been cold-shouldered by the Parisian
"élite." Cocteau was determined to "wake up," bestir and sing the praises of
the man who struck him as being like an "old sleeping oboe," and accordingly
asked Satie to work with him and Picasso for Diaghilev's Ballets russes.
The outcome would be *Parade*, which was a "*succès de scandale.*"

Erik Satie and Valentine Gross photographed by Cocteau,
at his home, August 1916. Satie has borrowed a sun hat from Cocteau.
Valentine was to remain the close confident of both composer and poet,
who felt mutual affection and annoyance towards one another, depending
on the day. With Picasso, on the other hand, Satie got on wonderfully well,
and even went so far as to say he was "proud of being his pupil."

Jeudi — 14 Sept 1916

Chère & douce Amie — Très gentille, votre lettre. Merci — Si vous saviez combien je suis triste : "Parade" se transforme, en mieux, derrière Cocteau! Picasso a des idées qui me plaisent mieux que celles de notre Jean! Quel malheur! Et je "suis" pour Picasso! Et Cocteau ne le sait pas! Que faire! Picasso me dit de continuer sur le texte de Jean,

& lui Picasso travaillera sur un autre texte, le sien — qui est étourdissant! Prodigieux! Je deviens fou & triste! Que faire! Connaissant les belles idées de Picasso, je suis navré d'être obligé de composer sur celles du bon Jean, moins belles — oh! oui! moins belles. Que faire! Que faire! — Écrivez-moi pour me conseiller. Je suis fou — Mille choses à Stein. Tout plein bonjour à vous

Letter from Satie to Valentine Gross, September 14, 1916.

Rag-time, an extract from Erik Satie's *Parade*, published by Rouart, Lerolle, 1919.

List of mechanical noises in a draft notebook for *Parade*, April 1917.
Parade would cause an outcry because of Picasso's daring sets
(circus horse, cardboard giants . . .) and Satie's score which included,
in particular, the first use of rag-time in European music, as well as sounds
made by typewriters, ships' sirens, pistol shots . . .

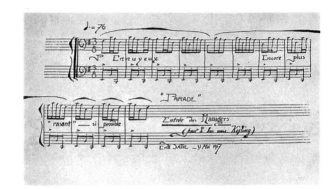

Extract from the score of *Parade* used to illustrate the program of a concert organized as a tribute to Erik Satie in the Salle Huyghens in June 1917. This was a riposte to the way the critics panned *Parade* and the audience's scandalized reaction to it at its première.

Michel Georges-Michel, *The Première of "Parade" at the Théâtre du Châtelet in 1917*. From right to left in the central box, Marie Laurencin, Diaghilev, Misia Edwards, Satie, Picasso, Cocteau and Michel Georges-Michel.

FESTIVAL ERICK SATIE
LUNDI 7 JUIN 1920

1 CONFÉRENCE SUR ERICK SATIE
PAR M. Jean Cocteau

2 PARADE (1917) Pour piano quatre mains (✱)
MLLE GERMAINE TAILLEFER ET L'AUTEUR

3 Trois petites pièces montées (1920) POUR ORCHESTRE (✱ ✱)
A) DE L'ENFANCE DE PANTAGRUEL (RÉVERIE)
B) MARCHE DE COCAGNE (DÉMARCHE)
C) JEUX DE GARGANTUA (COIN DE POLKA)

4 1ÈRE GYMNOPÉDIE (1888) (✱)
2ÈME SARABANDE (1887) (✱)
3ÈME GNOSSIENNE (1890) (✱)

TROIS NOCTURNES   (PREMIÈRE AUDITION)
CHAPITRES TOURNÉS EN TOUS SENS (1913) (✱ ✱ ✱)
A) CELLE QUI PARLE TROP;
B) LE PORTEUR DE GROSSES PIERRES;
C) LE REGRET DES ENFERMÉS
M. RICARDO VINES

5 SOCRATE (1920) DRAME SYMPHONIQUE POUR 4 SOPRANI & ORCHESTRE (✱ ✱)
(1ÈRE AUDITION AVEC ORCHESTRE) MME MARIA FREUND ET L'ORCHESTRE
L'ORCHESTRE SOUS LA DIRECTION DE M. FÉLIX DELGRANGE

PIANO ERARD

(✱) CHEZ ROUART ET LEROLLE (✱ ✱) AUX ÉDITIONS DE LA SIRÈNE
(✱ ✱ ✱) CHEZ DEMETS

Program of the *Festival Erik Satie*, 1920, based on a layout by Picasso.

Pablo Picasso, *Portrait of Erik Satie*, 1920.

Lundi soir.

Bon Vieil Homme noir —
Toi, ton cœur tout blanc.

Moi t'aime.

CRÂNE-POLI

Letter from Satie to Cocteau, October 23, 1917.

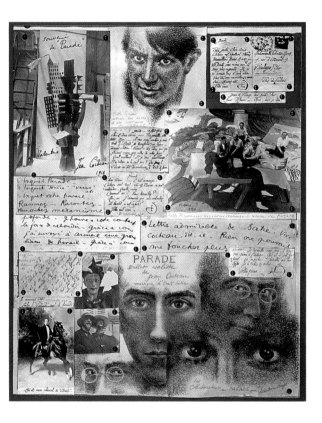

The team which created "Parade," montage by Valentine Hugo, 1916-1965.

Michel Larionov, *Wings of the Ballets russes*, 1917 - 1923.
From left to right, Stravinsky, Diaghilev, Cocteau brandishing a razor
[*raser* means both to shave and to bore] and Satie preparing
shaving soap. "Cocteau is still busy with his 'boring' 1917 stuff," Satie
wrote to Valentine Hugo at the time of a restaging of *Parade* in 1920.
"He 'bores' us, Picasso and me, and I can't take any more of it."

Pablo Picasso, *After Lunch*, November 21, 1919. From left to right,
Cocteau, Olga Picasso, Satie and Clive Bell, editor of *The Little Review* which
would publish writings by Satie and Cocteau.

The Good Master

"*There is no Satie school.
Satism could never exist.
I would be dead against it.
In art, there must be
no slavery.*"
Erik Satie

A ERIK SATIE, MON
MAITRE DE SACESSE.

Jean Cocteau dedicated his essay on Picasso, written in 1923,
to Erik Satie. Draft of this dedication on the title page of the manuscript.
Page 125: Francis Picabia, *The Good Master*.

Erik Satie, 1923.

Erik Satie

Conférence sur les "Six".

Mesdames, ... Messieurs, ... Mesdemoiselles .....

.....

Combien je suis heureux d'avoir à parler, ... ici, ... de mes jeunes amis "Les Six" ...
.....

Malgré leur jeunesse, .. il se trouve que j'ai pour eux une vieille amitié' ....

... Peut-être ... est-ce hors ce que j'ai eu le plaisir, .. il y a quelques années, .. de les avoir un peu présentés au public ...

.....

Avec eux, j'ai partagé de grandes joies ......

...... Ensemble, ... nous avons subi les attaques des mêmes adversaires; ...

... nous avons été soutenus par les mêmes amateurs; .... nous avons eu, .. devant nous, ... les mêmes critiques .....

.....

Tout cela, ... c'est quelque chose — quelque chose d'agréable — surtout pour moi ....

.....

....

Lecture on the Six, an extract from Satie's handwritten manuscript, 1921.

Looking through a window, at a friend's house, Satie discovered
the music of an unknown young composer, Darius Milhaud. Drawing by
Gea Augsbourg published in *La Vie de Darius Milhaud en images*, Corréa, 1935.

Cocteau introduces the Six to Erik Satie, drawing by Jean Oberlé, which appeared in
Le Crapouillot, 1921. It was, in fact, thanks to the composer of *Parade* that Cocteau
met the young composers Auric, Durey, Honegger, Milhaud, Poulenc and Germaine
Tailleferre, whom he would launch at the beginning of the Roaring Twenties under
the label of the *Groupe des Six*. This merry band, which drew its inspiration from

Satie's aesthetics – simplicity and absence of hierarchy among genres –
would become the darling of Paris. One of its more glorious moments was a teatro
buffo performance, organized by the actor and director Pierre Bertin, in which the
creative works included, among others, *Le Piège de Méduse*, written in 1913, which
represented an astonishing harbinger of Dada theater and the Theater of the Absurd.

Erik Satie and Pierre Bertin at Fontainebleau, by the Carp Pond, 1922.

Poster for the *Spectacle de Théâtre Bouffe*, Michel Theatre, May 1921.
Plays by Max Jacob, Satie, Cocteau and Radiguet; music by Auric,
Milhaud, Poulenc and Satie.

LE
PIÈGE DE MÉDUSE

COMÉDIE LYRIQUE EN UN ACTE

DE

M. ÉRIK SATIE

AVEC MUSIQUE DE DANSE DU MÊME MONSIEUR

ORNÉE DE GRAVURES SUR BOIS

PAR

M. GEORGES BRAQUE

EDITIONS DE LA
GALERIE SIMON
29 bis, Rue d'Astorg
PARIS

Le Piège de Méduse by Erik Satie, "with dance music by the same gentleman," illustrated by Georges Braque, published by the Galerie Simon, 1921.

Receipts for royalty advances from the publishers Rouart, Lerolle, 1919.
Page 135: Erik Satie and cigar photographed by Francis Poulenc in about 1922.
Satie said: "My doctor has always advised me to smoke. He adds by way of further
advice: 'Smoke, my friend. If you don't, someone else will smoke in your place'."

Satie jotting in a notebook, 1923.

Satie and the young painter Jean Guérin, 1923. After Satie had set Plato's
Dialogues to music, his young friends compared him to Socrates.

Memo by Erik Satie for his introduction to *Socrate* at the home of Princess Edmond de Polignac, who commissioned this "symphonic drama," 1918.

Jacques Guérin, Satie, Madeleine and Michel Castaing in the country, 1923.

...Me voici dans ma 56ᵉ année ; — je suis donc quinquagénaire ....

...... Les Critiques me représentent comme étant drôle ....

.....Ce n'est pas vrai .....

...Je ne suis pas drôle ,... ni ne désire l'être ....

...Je suis un triste, ... un mélancolique, ... un "pleureur"— comme le saule — ce qui est bien assez bon pour moi..

Extract from the handwritten manuscript of *Préambule*,
a lecture given by Erik Satie at the opening of a concert of his works
given by the pianist Marcelle Meyer in 1922.

Satierik

« Erik is 'Satierik'. »
Francis Picabia

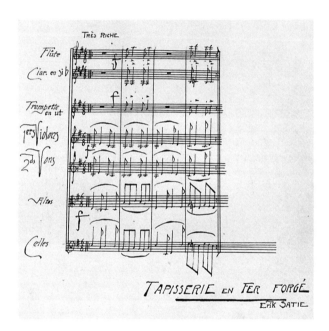

Erik Satie, *Tapisserie en fer forgé "pour l'arrivée des invités (grande réception),"*
1917-1923. Satie noted, before the spread of the radio, that people need
background noise for their everyday activities, so he came up with a
Musique d'ameublement, to be played so that "it cannot be heard."

1er Essai de "Musique d'Ameublement"
(Sons industriels)

Divertissement mobilier organisé par le groupe des musiciens "Nouveaux Jeunes" pour Jove, couturier-décorateur.

La Musique d'Ameublement, pour soirées, réunions, etc ... Ce qu'est la Musique d'ameublement? — un plaisir!
La Musique d'Ameublement remplace
les "valses",
les "fantaisies sur les opéras", etc....
Ne pas confondre! C'est autre chose!!!
Plus de "fausse musique": du meuble musical!
La Musique d'Ameublement complète le mobilier;
Elle permet Tout; Elle vaut de l'Or; elle est nouvelle; Elle ne dérange pas les habitudes;
Elle ne fatigue pas; Elle est Française; Elle est inusable; Elle n'ennuie pas.
L'adopter c'est faire mieux!
Écoutez sans vous gêner.

CONFECTION & SUR MESURE

Erik Satie, draft publicity handout for the *Musique d'ameublement*, 1918.
Page 143: Man Ray, *Erik Satie's Eyes*, "Rectified readymade," photo and matchbox. Tribute to the "only musician who had eyes."

Erik Satie photographed by Man Ray in 1922.

Poster for the *Soirée du Cœur à Barbe*, based on a layout by Naoum Granovski, 1923. During this evening, which was the arena for a famous squabble between Dadaists and future Surrealists, the *Trois morceaux en forme de poire* were played.

les
feuilles libres

J. GIRAUDOUX, DRIEU LA ROCHELLE, P. REVERDY,
Blaise CENDRARS, R. RADIGUET, Marcel RAVAL,
Erik SATIE, Georges AURIC, André LHOTE,
Roger de la FRESNAYE,

W. Mayr, Max Jacob, Benjamin Péret, J. Porel,
Francis Poulenc, Paul Fiérens, R.-M. Hermant,

ont collaboré

à ce

N° 27

Quatrième année   **3 fr.**   **Juin-Juillet 1922**

In the early 1920s, Satie collaborated with several
avant-garde literary reviews, including *Feuilles libres*, contributing his
Propos à propos and *Cahiers d'un Mammifère*.

Twenty years after the "sung waltzes" which had given
rise to their first meeting, Erik Satie and Paulette Darty were reunited
among mutual friends at Thimécourt in 1923.

Poster, based on a layout by Marcel-Louis Baugniet,
for a concert-lecture given by Satie in Brussels in March 1924.

anterne Sourde

upement Littéraire et Artistique
de l'Université de Bruxelles

AMEDI 15 MARS, à 8¹/₂ h. en la

AY (RUE ROYALE, 134)

SATIE

LA MUSIQUE

ivres seront interprétées par

LIA & Paul COLLAER

Pianiste

UWERYNS (36, rue du Treurenberg).

Téléphone 297.82

Much acclaimed by the Brussels avant-garde, Satie, in turn, introduced
several Belgian artists, including the young René Magritte, to Montparnasse.

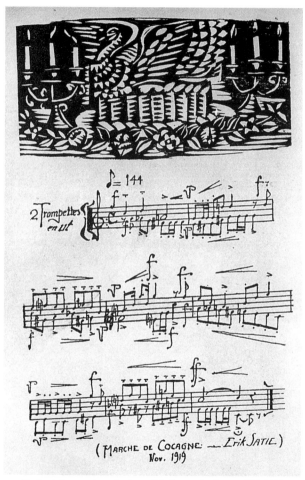

Marche de Cocagne, from the *Greasy Pole Almanac for the year 1920*, 1919.
Which would become, under the name of *Marche des Potassons*, the rallying call
for regulars at the Maison des Amis des Livres d'Adrienne Monnier.

Satie photographed by Man Ray, 1924.

Poster for a traveling Dada show in Holland, based on a layout
by Kurt Schwitters and Theo Van Doesburg. On it, the *Parade* rag-time
was announced under the title *Rag-time dada*.

Satie, photographed here by Brancusi in 1922, first dated his dedication of this photograph to Jean Wiener "1929" – four years after his own death!

SPORTS
&
DIVERTISSEMENTS.

MUSIQUE DE RIK. SATIE

DESSINS DE CH. MARTIN

PUBLICATIONS LUCIEN VOGEL, 11 RUE SAINT-FLORENTIN, PARIS

Frontispiece of Erik Satie's musical album *Sports & Divertissements*,
illustrated by Charles Martin. Published by Lucien Vogel, 1914-1923.
Opposite: Erik Satie playing golf on the St. Cloud course with
Henri-Pierre Roché, Jane Robert Foster and Brancusi.

Golf, extract from *Sports & Divertissement*, 1914.

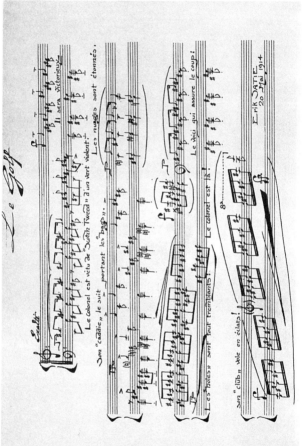

Erik Satie playing golf at St. Cloud with Brancusi, Henri-Pierre Roché, Jane Robert Foster and some caddies.

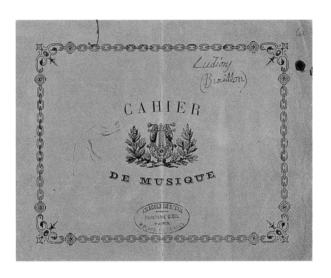

Musical notebook for the *Ludions*, five melodies composed
by Erik Satie on poems by Léon-Paul Fargue, for a masked ball given
by Count Etienne de Beaumont in 1923. "Something akin to *La Vida es Sueño*
by Calderon de la Barca," the pianist Ricardo Viñes would write, "seemed to be
echoed in the strange destiny of the Good Master of Arcueil who, in his endless
toing and froing between his dingy hovel and the luxurious salons of the capital,
had at times, in the face of this dual and hallucinatory existence, to wonder, like a
modern day Segismundo, where phantasmagoria lay, and where reality . . ."
*opposi*te: *On Hearing Satie*, print by Robert Bonfils which was published
in *Modes et Manières d'Aujourdhui*, 1920.

Arcueil-Cachan, le 3 jar 1921

Cher ami — Tous mes vœux cordiaux — (Cordial-Médoc.

J'ai une pensée pour votre journal :

— J'aimerais jouer avec un piano qui aurait une grosse queue —

Erik SATIE

Letter to Francis Picabia, editor of *391*, January 3, 1921.

Erik Satie's first dinner jacket, 1922.

Erik Satie by the poster for the *Soirées de Paris*, organized by
the Count de Beaumont at the Théâtre de la Cigale in the spring of 1924.
Photograph by René Clair, dedicated to his future wife, Bronia Perlmutter.

Erik Satie's notes for the score of *Mercure*,
"plastic poses" by Pablo Picasso and Léonide Massine,
created during the *Soirées de Paris* in June 1924.

Extract from a letter by Erik Satie to Marcel Raval,
editor of *Feuilles libres*, October 21, 1924. Satie joined forces with Picabia
for the ballet *Relâche* which was created in December for Rolf de Maré's
Swedish ballet company. In so doing he moved away from Satie and
the Six, whom he now deemed to be too "restrained".

Extract from the score of *Relâche*, 1924.

Maquette by Picabia for a sequence of *Relâche*: "The Men Get Undressed."

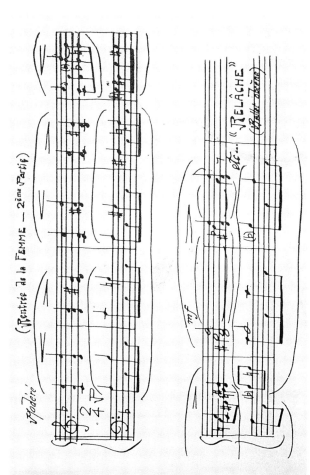

"The Woman's Return to the Stage," an extract from the score of *Relâche*, "obscene ballet." Satie claimed to have composed "pornographic" music because he had borrowed the tunes of bawdy songs (without the words, needless to add) for his score.

Pourquoi payer le luxe de votre fournisseur ou son ignorance ?

Pour être un penseur il faut penser.

Pourquoi payer votre fournisseur ou son ignorance ?

Das leben ist ein schöne abord.

Pourquoi payer le luxe ou son ignorance ?

Tout appel non justifié expose aux poursuites judiciaires et du Salon des Tuileries.

Pourquoi payer son ignorance.

C'est ainsi que les saintes images ont une vague odeur de fromage.

Pourquoi ?

Saviez-vous qu'il y a une Adaptation Française ?

E. L. T. MESENS

Le conscient est l'Évolution Dernière et Tardive du système organique, et par conséquent aussi, ce qu'il a dans ce système de moins achevé et de moins fort.

Un instantané et de

——+—— En rêve.

——+—— Les bordels font une impression très

——•—— On croirait entrer dans un Conserva

—— —— Les invalides justifient le cubisme.

Le pôle positif aime le pôle négatif, puisqu'on aime

J'aime la bière et les roses trémières.

Un homme en costume d'Adam.

Les chats sont heureux de vivre en dessou chaises.

La vache a du sentiment.

RENÉ MAGRITTE

LES BALLETS SUÉDOIS DONNERON

LE 27 NOVEMBRE

AU THÉÂTRE DES CHAMPS ÉLYSÉES

" RELÂCHE "

BALLET

INSTANTANÉISTE

EN DEUX ACTES, UN ENTR'ACTE CINÉMATOGRAPHIQUE

ET LA QUEUE DU CHIEN

PAR

FRANCIS PICABIA

MUSIQUE

D'

ERIK SATIE

CHORÉGRAPHIE DE JEAN BORLIN

Apportez des lunettes noires et de quoi vous boucher les oreilles.

RETENEZ VOS PLACES

Messieurs les ex-Dadas sont priés de venir manifester et surtout de crier : « A BAS SATIE ! A PICABIA ! VIVE LA NOUVELLE REVUE FRANCAISE ! »

" 391 "

N° 19

PRIX : 2 FRS

Dépositaire " AU SANS PAREIL "
37, Avenue Kléber, PARIS

Le Gérant, PIERRE DE MASSOT

Behind the *Journal de l'Instantanéisme* lurks the figure of Marcel Duchamp, friend of Satie's and *éminence grise* of this movement.

DAISME, INSTANTANÉISME

391

ournal de l'Instantanéisme

POUR QUELQUE TEMPS

NSTANTANÉISTE EST UN ÊTRE EXCEPTIONNEL
CYNIQUE ET INDÉCENT

LE SEUL MOUVEMENT C'EST
LE MOUVEMENT PERPÉTUEL !

L'INSTANTANÉISME : EST POUR
CEUX QUI ONT QUELQUE CHOSE A DIRE.

Dans son prochain nu-
méro "391" donnera une
liste des premiers Instan-
tanéistes, hommes excep-
tionnels.

IL N'Y A QU'UN MOUVEMENT
C'EST LE MOUVEMENT PERPÉTUEL !

L'INSTANTANÉISME : NE VEUT PAS D'HIER.
L'INSTANTANÉISME : NE VEUT PAS DE DEMAIN.
L'INSTANTANÉISME : FAIT DES ENTRECHATS.
L'INSTANTANÉISME : FAIT DES AILES DE PIGEONS.
L'INSTANTANÉISME : NE VEUT PAS DE GRANDS HOMMES.
L'INSTANTANÉISME : NE CROIT QU'A AUJOURD'HUI.
L'INSTANTANÉISME : VEUT LA LIBERTÉ POUR TOUS.
L'INSTANTANÉISME : NE CROIT QU'A LA VIE.
L'INSTANTANÉISME : NE CROIT QU'AU MOUVEMENT PERPÉTUEL.

The publicity for the "instantaneist" ballet *Relâche* recommended that the
audience come equipped with "dark glasses and something to plug the ears."

Jeudi 23 oct. 1924

Cher Monsieur Clair —— Et le film ?...
Quand ?... Le temps passe (& ne repasse pas)
Ai la "frousse" d'être oublié par vous . Oui...
Envoyez-moi rapidement le détail de votre si
merveilleux travail . Merci fort .
Bien vôtre , je suis

Letter from Erik Satie to René Clair, October 23, 1924.
Shortly before the creation of *Relâche*, Satie had still not seen either the film
prologue or the film interval of the ballet, shot by René Clair, for which
he had to compose the first "image-by-image" film music.

Left to right, René Clair, Satie, Picabia and his lady friend Germaine Everling
during the shooting of the interval in *Relâche*, 1924.

Shooting the interval of *Relâche*, on the terrace of the Théâtre des Champs-Elysées. From left to right, the star dancer of the Swedish Ballet Jean Börlin, Germaine Everling and Satie. At centre, by the camera, Picabia.

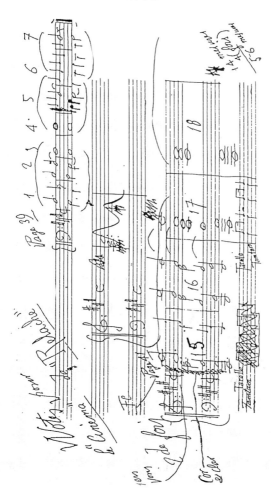

"Notes for the *Cinéma* of *Relâche*." Erik Satie's last score.

Picabia and Satie rehearsing the prologue of *Relâche*
in front of René Clair and Jean Börlin.

Erik Satie

For the prologue of *Relâche*, Satie and Picabia get ready to sound the three knocks – signaling that the curtain is about to go up – by firing the canon at the spectators.

Satie and his umbrella, in René Clair's *Entr'acte.*

In a sequence in *Entr'acte*, the Swedish dancer Inge Fries was made up "*à la Satie*."

Erik Satie's draft for a monument to himself,
with the following epitaph: "I came into the world very young in a very old era."
Opposite: Erik Satie's grave in the Arcueil cemetery.

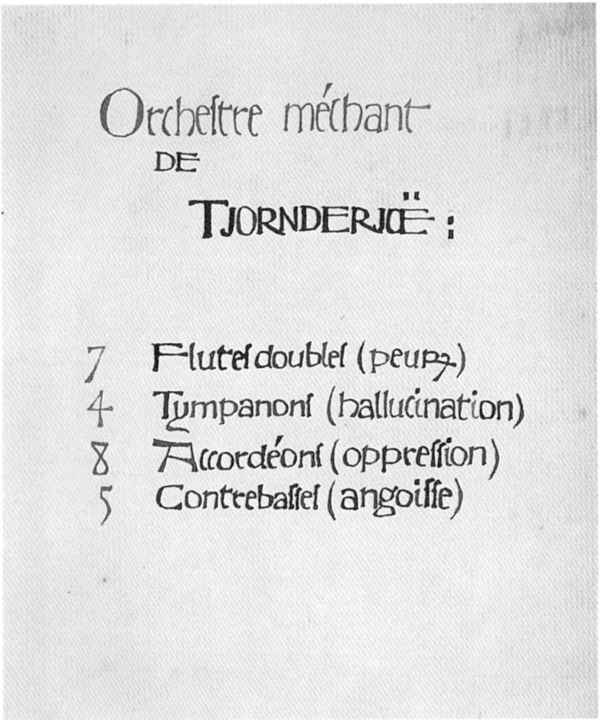

Orcheſtre méchant

DE

TJORNDERJŒ̈ ;

7   Fluteſdoubleſ (peurꝫ)
4   Tympanonſ (hallucination)
8   Accordéonſ (oppreſſion)
5   Contrebaſſeſ (angoiſſe)

Finely handwritten notes by Erik Satie, found in his room in Arcueil.

GRAND CINQ-MATS
« L'ÉTOILE »
EXCURSIONS POLAIRES

Auberge du Pot Rouge

After Erik Satie's death, on July 1, 1925 at St. Joseph's Hospital, his legend – which he himself had helped to perpetuate – went from strength to strength. One of his last disciples, Henri Sauguet from the school at Arcueil, would have the same dream several times over. He met up once more with his Good Master in heaven. Strangely attired in the once young Velvet Gentleman's suit, Satie beckoned to him to approach and then whispered in his ear: "Tell me, my friend, do they still think I'm dead, down there?"

Francis Picabia, illustration for the score of *Relâche*, Rouart, Lerolle, 1926.
One of the characters in the ballet (in the sequence "The Men get Undressed")
comes to heaven to pay his respects to Satie. Sitting on a cloud, Satie holds up
a notice with the words: "When will we break the habit of explaining everything?"

Appendices

Title list: an English version

In the literature, Satie's works are invariably referred to only by their French titles. These suggested – and in no way definitive – translations are included merely to illustrate this aspect of the composer's wit, for English readers. Only these titles mentioned in the text have been included.

Airs à faire fuir: scary airs

Cahiers d'un Mammifère:
a mammal's notebook

Ce que je suis: what I am

Danses de travers: crooked dances

En Habit de Cheval: in horse dress

Instant musical: musical split second

Je te veux: I want you

La Belle Excentrique: the eccentric belle

Le Fils des étoiles: son of the stars

Le Piège de Méduse: Medusa's trap

Marche de Cocagne: greasy pole march

Marche des Potassons:
march of the plump

Mémoires d'un amnésique:
memoirs of an amnesic

Mercure: Mercury

Messe des pauvres: paupers' mass

Musique d'ameublement:
furnishing music

*Neuvaine pour la fort tranquillité
de mon âme*: novena for the deep
tranquillity of my soul

Ogives: diagonal arches

Préambule: preamble

Propos à propos: apposite remarks

Relâche: no performance

Socrate: Socrates

Sonneries de la Rose+Croix:
rosicrucian chimes

Sports & Divertissements:
sports and entertainment

Tapisserie en fer forgé "pour l'arrivée
des invités (grande réception)":
wrought iron wallpaper "for the arrival
of guests (grand reception)"

Trois morceaux en forme de poire:
three pear-shaped pieces

*Véritables préludes flasques
(pour un chien)*: real limp preludes
(for a dog)

Verset laïque et somptueux:
lay and lavish versicle

Bibliography

Musical works

For solo piano

Gymnopédies, 1888. Salabert.

Ogives, 1889. Chant du Monde.

Gnossiennes, 1889-1897. Salabert.

Sonneries de la Rose+Croix, 1892. Salabert.

Le Fils des étoiles, 1892. Salabert.

Danses gothiques, « neuvaine pour la fort tranquillité de mon âme, » 1893. Salabert.

Vexations, 1893. Max Eschig.

Prélude de « La Porte héroïque du ciel, » 1894. Salabert.

Pièces froides: Airs à faire fuir; Danses de travers, 1897. Salabert.

Jack in the Box, 1899. Universal.

Poudre d'or, 1902. Salabert.

Prélude en tapisserie, 1906. Salabert.

Véritables préludes flasques (pour un chien), 1912. Max Eschig.

Sept toutes petites danses pour « Le Piège de Méduse, » 1913. Salabert.

Descriptions automatiques, 1913. Max Eschig.

Embryons desséchés, 1913. Max Eschig.

Croquis & Agaceries d'un gros bonhomme en bois, 1913. Max Eschig.

Chapitres tournés en tous sens, 1913. Max Eschig.

L'Enfance de Ko-Quo, 1913. Inédit.

Menus propos enfantins; Enfantillages pittoresques; Peccadilles importunes, 1913. Max Eschig.

Vieux sequins & vieilles cuirasses, 1913. Max Eschig.

Sports & Divertissements, 1914. Salabert.

Les Trois Valses distinguées du précieux dégoûté, 1914. Salabert.

Heures séculaires et instantanées, 1914. Max Eschig.

Avant-dernières pensées, 1915. Salabert.

Nocturnes, 1919: I; II; III, Salabert. IV; V; VI, Max Eschig.

For four-handed piano duet

Trois morceaux en forme de poire, 1903. Salabert.

Aperçus désagréables, 1908-1912. Max Eschig.

For piano and violin

Choses vues à droite & à gauche (sans lunettes), 1914. Salabert.

Embarquement pour Cythère, 1917. Salabert.

For voice and piano

*Cinq mélodies de 1886: Élégie;
Les Anges; Sylvie; Les Fleurs; Chanson,*
poésies de J.-P. Contamine de Latour.
Salabert.

Geneviève de Brabant, musique de
scène pour la pièce en vers et en prose
en trois actes de Lord Cheminot,
vers 1900. Universal.

Je te veux, paroles d'Henry Pacory,
1897. Salabert.

*Neuf chansons de cabaret et de
caf'conc',* 1899-1905: *Un dîner
à l'Élysée; Le Veuf; Petit recueil des fêtes:
Le picador est mort; Sorcière; Enfant-
martyre; Air fantôme,* paroles
de Vincent Hyspa; *Imperial-Oxford,*
d'après Contamine de Latour;
J'avais un ami, paroles d'Erik Satie?;
La Chemise, paroles de Jules Dépaquit.
Salabert.

La Diva de « L'Empire », paroles
de Dominique Bonnaud et Numa Blès,
1904. Salabert.

Trois poèmes d'amour, paroles
d'Erik Satie, 1914. Salabert.

*Trois mélodies de 1916: Statue de
bronze,* poème de Léon-Paul Fargue;
Daphénéo, paroles de M. God;
Le Chapelier, paroles de René Chalupt
d'après *Alice au pays des merveilles.*
Salabert.

*Quatre petites mélodies:
Élégie à la mémoire de Debussy,*
poème de Lamartine; *Danseuse,*
poésie de Jean Cocteau; *Chanson,*
texte anonyme du XVIIIᵉ siècle;
Adieu, poésie de Raymond Radiguet,
1920. Max Eschig.

Chœur de marins, paroles de
Jean Cocteau et Raymond Radiguet
extraites de l'opéra-comique
Paul et Virginie, 1921. Salabert.

For choir and organs

Messe des pauvres, 1895. Salabert.

For small ensemble

*Musique d'ameublement: Carrelage
phonique; Tapisserie en fer forgé;
Tenture de cabinet préfectoral,*
1917-1923. Salabert.

For orchestra

En habit de cheval, 1911. Salabert.

Parade, « ballet réaliste. »
Thème de Jean Cocteau, décors
de Pablo Picasso, 1917. Salabert.

*Cinq grimaces pour « Le Songe
d'une nuit d'Été, »* 1915. Universal.

Trois petites pièces montées, 1920.
Max Eschig.

La Belle Excentrique, « fantaisie
sérieuse, » 1920. Max Eschig.

Mercure, « poses plastiques »
de Pablo Picasso, 1924. Universal.

Relâche, « ballet instantanéiste. »
Thème et décors de Francis Picabia,
1924. Salabert.

Cinéma, entracte symphonique
de *Relâche.* Cinématographie de
René Clair, 1924. Salabert.

For voice and orchestra

Socrate, « drame symphonique, »
d'après les Dialogues de Platon, traduits
par Victor Cousin, 1918. Max Eschig.

Writings

Le Piège de Méduse, « comédie lyrique
d'Erik Satie avec musique de danse du
même Monsieur, » 1913, Paris, Galerie
Simon, 1921; Le Castor astral, 1988.

Écrits, collected and introduced by
Ornella Volta, Paris, Champ libre, 1977 ;
Gérard Lebovici/Ivréa, 1981 and 1990.

Quaderni di un Mammifero, collected by
Ornella Volta, Milan, Adelphi, 1980.

Schriften, collected and introduced by Ornella Volta, Hofheim, Wolke, 1988.

Les Bulles du Parcier, collected and introduced by Ornella Volta, Montpellier, Bibliothèque artistique et littéraire, 1991.

Briefe 1 and *2*, collected and introduced by Ornella Volta, Hofheim, Wolke, 1991 and 1997.

A Mammal's Notebook, collected and introduced by Ornella Volta, London, Atlas Press, 1996.

Monographs on Erik Satie

Pierre-Daniel Templier, *Erik Satie*, Paris, Rieder, 1932; Les Éditions d'Aujourd'hui, 1975.

Rollo Myers, *Erik Satie*, London, Denis Dobson, 1948; New York, Dover, 1968.

Grete Wehmeyer, *Erik Satie*, Ratisbonne, Gustav Bosse, 1974.

Anne Rey, *Erik Satie*, Paris, Le Seuil/Solfèges, 1974 and 1995.

James Harding, *Erik Satie*, London, Secker & Warburg, 1975.

Ornella Volta, *L'Ymagier d'Erik Satie*, Paris, Opéra de Paris/Francis Van de Velde, 1979 and 1989.

Adriana Guarnieri Corazzol, *Erik Satie tra ricerca e provocazione*, Venice, Marsilio, 1979.

Vincent Lajoinie, *Erik Satie*, Lausanne, L'Âge d'Homme, 1985.

Alan M. Gillmor, *Erik Satie*, Boston, Twayne, 1988; New York-London, W. W. Norton, 1992.

Ornella Volta, *Satie seen through his letters*, with a preface by John Cage, London and New York, Marion Boyars, 1989.

Robert Orledge, *Satie the Composer*, Cambridge, Cambridge University Press, 1990.

Ornella Volta, *Satie et la danse*, Paris, Plume, 1992.

Ornella Volta, *Erik Satie: Bibliographie raisonnée*, Arcueil, Mairie d'Arcueil and Archives de la Fondation Erik Satie, 1995.

Robert Orledge, *Satie remembered*, London, Faber & Faber, 1996.

Ludwig Striegel, *Satierik Paedagogus?*, with a preface by Rudolf-Dieter Kraemer, Augsbourg, Forum Musikpädagogik no. 19, 1996.

Exhibition catalogues

Erik Satie, by François Lesure, Paris-Arcueil, Bibliothèque nationale, 1966.

Satie op papier, by Ad Petersen and Dorine Mignot, with a preface by Ornella Volta, Amsterdam, Stedelijk Museum, 1976.

Erik Satie e gli artisti del nostro tempo, by Ornella Volta, Spoleto, Galleria nazionale d'Arte moderna et Festival dei Due Mondi, 1981.

Erik Satie et la tradition populaire, by Ornella Volta, Paris, Fondation Erik Satie at the Musée national des arts et traditions populaires, 1988.

Erik Satie del Chat Noir a Dada, by Ornella Volta, Valencia, IVAM, 1996.

Discography

All the four handed piano duets,
with just one or two exceptions,
have been recorded by:

Jean-Pierre Armengaud, for
Mandala/Harmonia Mundi.

Jean-Joël Barbier, for La Boîte
à Musique.

Aldo Ciccolini, for EMI.

France Clidat, for Forlane.

Olof Höjer, for Prophone.

Aki Takahashi, for EMI-Japon.

Anthologies
have been recorded by:

Klara Körmendi, for Naxos.

Reinbert de Leeuw,
for Philips.

Joanna Mc Gregor, for Collins.

Anne Queffelec,
for Virgin Classic.

Pascal Rogé, for Decca.

Yitkin Séow, for Hyperion.

Riri Shimada, for CBS/Sony.

Gabriel Tacchino,
for Pierre Vérany.

Yuji Takahashi, for Denon.

Daniel Varsano, for CBS.

The complete works piano duet
have been recorded by:

Jean-Pierre Armengaud and Dominique
Merlet, for Mandala/Harmonia Mundi.

Philippe Corre and Édouard Exerjean,
for Pierre Vérany.

Le Duo Campion/Vachon, for Analekta.

Works for orchestra
have been recorded by:

Maurice Abravanel, Utah Symphony
Orchestra, for Vanguard.

Philippe Entremont, Royal
Philharmonic Orchestra, for CBS.

Bernard Hermann, London Festival
Players, for Decca.

Michel Plasson, Orchestre du Capitole
de Toulouse, for EMI.

Manuel Rosenthal, Orchestre national
de France, for Adès.

**The melodies and songs for cabaret
and/or café-concert,**
which form two almost complete
"collections," have been recorded by:

Yumi Nara, Jeff Cohen on piano,
for Fontec.

Anne-Marie Schmidt, Jean-Pierre Armengaud on piano, for Mandala.

Some of these melodies and songs have been recorded, among others, by:

Gabriel Bacquier, Nicolaï Gedda and Mady Mesplé, Aldo Ciccolini on piano, for EMI.

Cathy Berbarian, Dario Müller on piano, for Ermitage.

Régine Crespin, Philippe Entremont on piano, for Philips.

Felicity Lott, Graham Johnson on piano, for Forlane.

Jessie Norman, Dalton Baldwin on piano, for Philips.

No recording of the quite separate work Socrate is satisfactory in the version for four sopranos, as intended by Satie. For the version for voice and piano, however, there is the recording of Hugues Cuenod, accompanied on the piano by Geoffrey Parsons, for Nimbus, and, for the version for voice and orchestra, the recording of Jean-Paul Fauchécourt with the Erwartung Ensemble, conducted by Bernard Desgraupes, for FNAC Music, despite the fact that this is an adaptation of the original score.

Miscellaneous works

Vexations, the work for piano with a single musical motif followed by two variations, to be repeated 840 times in succession, has been recorded twice: for Philips, by Reinbert de Leeuw, requiring that the record containing thirty consecutive recordings is replaced twenty-eight times on the player; for Decca, by Alan Marks, who presents his forty

consecutive recordings as an "extract" from a work which, if played in its entirety, would have filled twenty-one CDs.

Three Musiques d'ameublement plus Cinéma (music for the film Entracte) have been recorded for Erato by the Ars Nova Ensemble, conducted by Marius Constant.

The EMI 78 rpm record, re-recorded on CD, Les Inspirations insolites d'Erik Satie, includes, in addition to rarely played works such as Geneviève de Brabant and the Messe des pauvres, the "lyrical comedy" Le Piège de Méduse, played by Pierre Bertin, who created this piece in the presence of the author, in 1921. Conducted by Aldo Ciccolini.

The highly personalized instructions which Satie slipped in between the staffs intended just for his performer, who was forbidden to read them aloud during the performance, have nevertheless been recorded by:

Raymond Devos, accompanied on the piano by Michel Legrand, for Erato.

Caroline Gautier, accompanied on the piano by William Nabore, for MPO/Misidisc.

Jeanne Moreau, accompanied on the piano by Jean-Marc Luisada, for Deutsche Grammophon.

Claude Piéplu, accompanied on the piano by Jean-Pierre Armengaud, for Circé-Adda.

Not forgetting

Those interested in hearing the pianists whom Satie knew and appreciated him-